LIKE ME LIKE YOU

Zack has ASTHMA

JILLIAN POWELL

Evans

Hi, my name is
Zack and I have
asthma. It means
I sometimes find it
hard to breathe.
The doctors found
out I had asthma
when I was
very young.

6

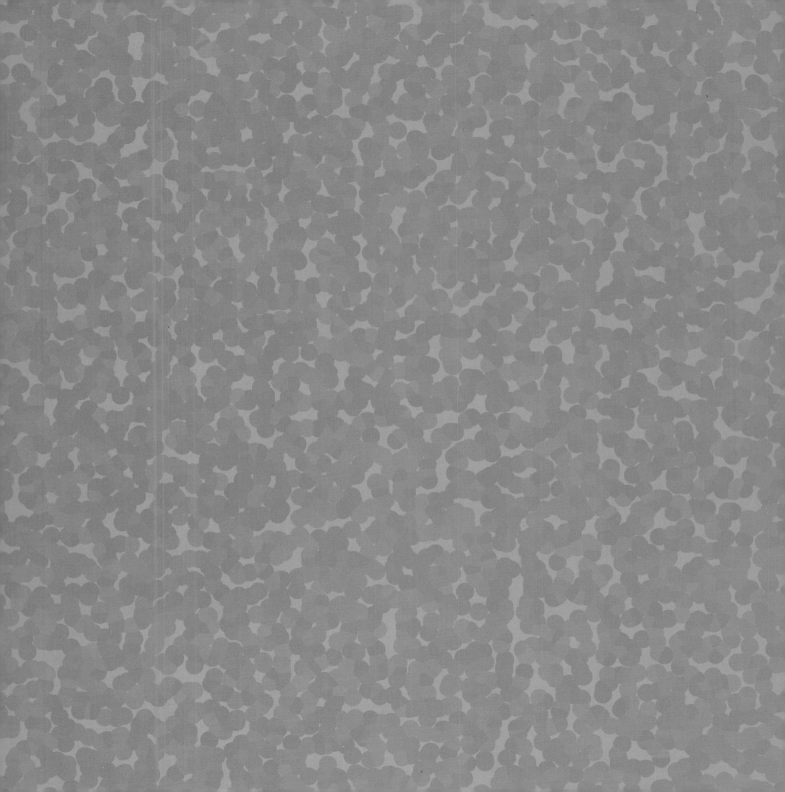

First published in paperback in 2009
by Evans Brothers Limited
2A Portman Mansions
Chiltern Street
London W1U 6NR

Printed in China

British Library Cataloguing in Publication data.

Powell, Jillian
Zack has asthma. - (Like Me, Like You)
1. Astham - Juvenile literature 2. Asthmatics - Juvenile literature
I. Title
618.9'2238

ISBN 9780237538613

Acknowledgements

The author and publishers would like to thank the following for their help with this book:

Zack, Ryan, Carleigh and Debi Cullen, Chris Jordan, Mick Hill and the under-nine's Thanet Colts football team.

Thanks also to The National Asthma Campaign for their help in the preparation of this book.

All photographs by Gareth Boden, except p.27, courtesy of Patrick Ladbury and The National Asthma Campaign and p.7, courtesy of Argos.

Credits

Series Editor: Louise John
Editor: Julia Bird
Designer: Mark Holt
Production: Jenny Mulvanny

ASTHMA

Asthma makes the **airways** to the lungs narrower so it is harder to breathe.

I live with my mum, brother and sister. They all have asthma too. We keep some fish as pets. I would like to have a dog, but we can't, because animal **dander** can make our asthma worse.

7

We live near the sea. We often go for walks along the beach, and I sometimes play football there too. I like being out in the fresh air.

ASTHMA TRIGGERS

Infections like colds
Dirty air or smoke
House-dust mites
Plant pollen
Animal dander (flakes of skin and saliva)
Changes in the weather

We have to be careful to keep our house clean, because the **mites** that live in **house dust** are very bad for our asthma. We all take turns at cleaning and vacuuming!

I have special covers on my bed to keep house-dust mites away. Mum vacuums the bed once a week, too.

She also puts all my sheets and pillow cases in a very hot wash to kill any house-dust mites.

HOUSE-DUST MITES

House-dust mites are very small and can only be seen through a **microscope**. This picture shows a house-dust mite enlarged to more than a thousand times its real size!

11

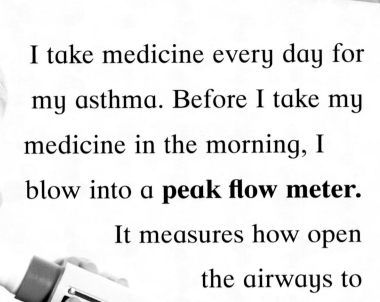

I take medicine every day for my asthma. Before I take my medicine in the morning, I blow into a **peak flow meter.** It measures how open the airways to my lungs are. I take a deep breath in, then blow out hard into the meter. I blow into the meter three times.

Then I write down my highest level on a chart. I show the chart to the nurse when I go for a check-up at the asthma clinic. I have a check-up four times a year. The nurse listens to my breathing, weighs and measures me and checks that I'm using my **inhaler** properly.

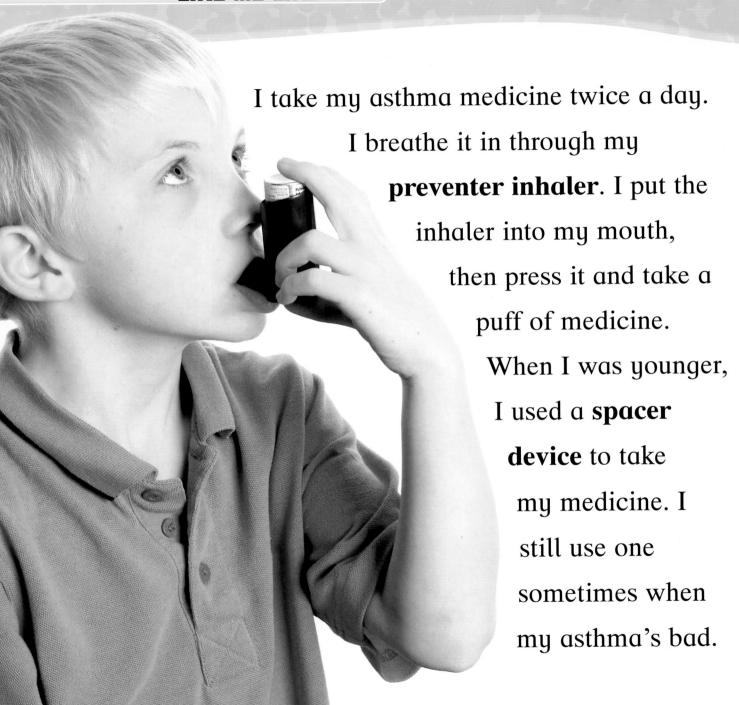

I take my asthma medicine twice a day. I breathe it in through my **preventer inhaler**. I put the inhaler into my mouth, then press it and take a puff of medicine. When I was younger, I used a **spacer device** to take my medicine. I still use one sometimes when my asthma's bad.

After I use my inhaler, I clean my teeth and wash out my mouth in case there is any medicine left in it. I have to remember to take my medicine again at night before I go to bed.

Today I'm going to play football for my team. I pack my **reliever inhaler** in my sports bag. I use this inhaler when my asthma's bad. It contains medicine that helps me breathe more easily. I take my reliever inhaler everywhere I go and keep a spare one in my desk at school.

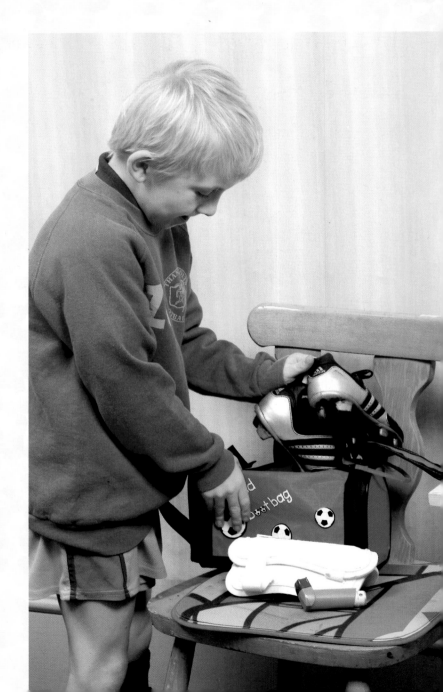

I love football and my favourite team is Manchester United. My own football team won a trophy this year, because we came second out of twenty-four teams!

Today we're playing against a team from a nearby town. I'm playing in defence. It's hard work but I really enjoy it!

After a while, I start to feel a bit wheezy. The coach makes me a sub so I can have a rest. The grass has been cut and that makes my asthma worse. My chest feels tight and I'm coughing.

ALLERGIES

Many children who have asthma also have **allergies** such as **hay fever** or food allergies.

19

I have to use my reliever inhaler. It's a different colour from the preventer inhaler, so I don't get them mixed up. I'm using a spacer device with the inhaler to help get the medicine to my lungs more quickly.

It takes about ten minutes for the reliever medicine to work. My team-mates Robert and Matthew come over at half-time to ask how I'm feeling.

21

Mum asks me if I'm feeling a bit better now. She can also tell if I'm getting better by feeling my back to see if my breathing is getting easier.

ONE IN EIGHT

About one in eight children have asthma.

After a while, the wheezing stops and I feel ready to join in the game again. I wait with the coach until it's time to go back on to the pitch.

I'm always really hungry after playing football! At home, Mum makes us a snack while I tell my sister Carleigh all about the match.

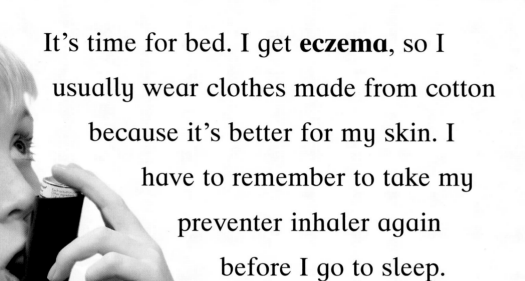

It's time for bed. I get **eczema**, so I usually wear clothes made from cotton because it's better for my skin. I have to remember to take my preventer inhaler again before I go to sleep.

ECZEMA

Eczema is common in children who have asthma. It's a skin condition that causes itching and rashes.

25

The worst thing about having asthma is when it's bad and I have to rest. But most of the time, I can do what I like. I love running, playing football and doing other sports.

The best thing is going on special holidays for children with asthma! We always have lots of fun and it's great making friends with other children who have asthma too.

Some children grow out of asthma when they reach their teens.

Glossary

Airways the tubes that carry air into and out of the lungs

Allergies when the body reacts badly to a trigger such as food, pollen or dust

Asthma a condition that can cause problems with breathing, such as coughing and wheezing

Dander flakes of skin and saliva

Eczema a condition that causes a rash and itching. It can be an allergy

Hay fever allergy caused by plant pollen

House-dust mites small creatures that live in household dust

Inhaler something that is used to breathe medicine into the lungs

Microscope an instrument which makes things look bigger then they are

Peak flow meter a meter which measures how open the airways to the lungs are

Preventer asthma medicine taken every day to try to prevent asthma

Reliever medicine which helps make breathing easier when asthma has started

Spacer device a plastic container which fits over the mouth and makes it easier to use an inhaler

Index

Further Information

UNITED KINGDOM
Asthma UK
Tel: 08457 01 02 03/adviceline
www.asthma.org.uk
UK charity working together to improve the lives
of people with asthma.

The British Allergy Foundation
Tel. 01322 619898
www.allergyfoundation.com
Offers lots of information and support for asthma
and many kinds of allergies.

UNITED STATES OF AMERICA
American Lung Association
www.lungusa.org
Lots of facts and information on asthma
including asthma in children.

AUSTRALIA
National Asthma Council
Tel: (03) 9929 4333
www.nationalasthma.org.au
Support and guidance for asthma sufferers.

BOOKS
Asthma (Feeling Ill?), Jillian Powell,
Evans 2007

Asthma (How's Your Health?), Angela Royston,
Franklin Watts 2006

My Friend has Asthma, Anna Levene,
Chrysalis Children's Books 2003

Asthma (It's not catching), Angela Royston,
Heinemann Library 2005